The Life Cycle of a

TREE

John Williams

Illustrated by
Jackie Harland

Reading Consultant:
Diana Bentley

The Bookwright Press
New York · 1989

Life Cycles

The Life Cycle of an Ant
The Life Cycle of a Butterfly
The Life Cycle of a Frog
The Life Cycle of a Rabbit

The Life Cycle of a Stickleback
The Life Cycle of a Sunflower
The Life Cycle of a Swallow
The Life Cycle of a Tree

First published in the
United States in 1989 by
The Bookwright Press
387 Park Avenue South
New York, NY 10016

First published in 1988 by
Wayland (Publishers) Limited
61 Western Road, Hove
East Sussex, BN3 1JD, England

Library of Congress Cataloging-in-Publication Data
Williams, John.
   The life cycle of a tree/by John Williams; illustrated by
Jackie Harland; reading consultant, Diana Bentley.
      p. cm.—(Life cycles)
   Bibliography: p.
   Includes index.
   Summary: Describes, using the chestnut tree as an
example, the growth and life of a tree from seed to
maturity.
   ISBN 0-531-18259-2
   1. Trees—Life cycle—Juvenile literature.   2. Chestnut—
Life cycle—Juvenile literature.   (1. Trees—Life cycle.
2. Chestnut—Life cycle.)   I. Harland, Jackie, ill.   II. Title.
III. Series.
QK475.8.W55 1989
583'.976—dc 19   88-5955
                                                                            CIP
                                                                            AC

Typeset in the UK by DP Press Limited, Sevenoaks, Kent
Printed by Casterman S.A., Belgium

Notes for parents and teachers
Each title in this series has been specially written and
designed as a first natural history book for young readers.
For less able readers there are introductory captions,
while the more detailed text explains each illustration.

Contents

All the words that are
in **bold** are explained in
the glossary on page 31.

This is a chestnut tree.

Look at this huge tree. It is called a chestnut tree. Chestnut trees can grow as tall as a house. They have long, spiky leaves and twisted **bark**. In the summer, flowers grow on the chestnut tree.

5

6

Chestnut trees grow flowers and **burs.**

The flowers make the chestnut fruit. The fruit has a hard case with lots of prickly spikes. This is called a bur. Inside the bur, there will be up to three chestnuts. The chestnuts are the seeds that will grow into new trees.

Male and female chestnut flowers.

In the summer, flowers grow on the chestnut tree. These flowers are called **catkins**. There are two kinds of catkin flowers, the male and the female. The male flowers grow in groups along the length of the catkin. The female flowers grow at the base of the catkin.

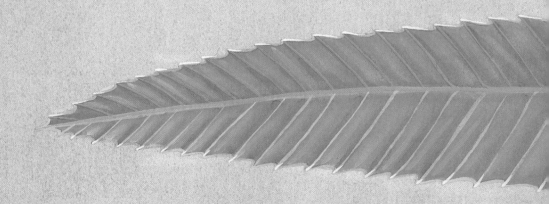

9

Pollen is taken from the male flowers to the female.

The male flowers make a yellow powder called pollen. The pollen has to get to the female flowers to make the fruit grow. Insects like chestnut pollen. They will visit many catkins. Pollen brushes off the insects' legs and body onto the female flowers. This is called **pollination**.

The seeds can begin to grow.

The pollen that has been carried by the insects will brush off onto the parts of the female flower that will form the new seeds. This is called **fertilization**. Now the chestnuts will begin to grow inside each bur. The male flowers wither and die.

13

14

The chestnuts grow inside the bur.

The chestnuts grow inside their green, spiky burs. These hard cases protect the chestnuts from bad weather and creatures that might eat them. By the autumn the chestnuts are ready to come out of the burs. They are full-grown seeds.

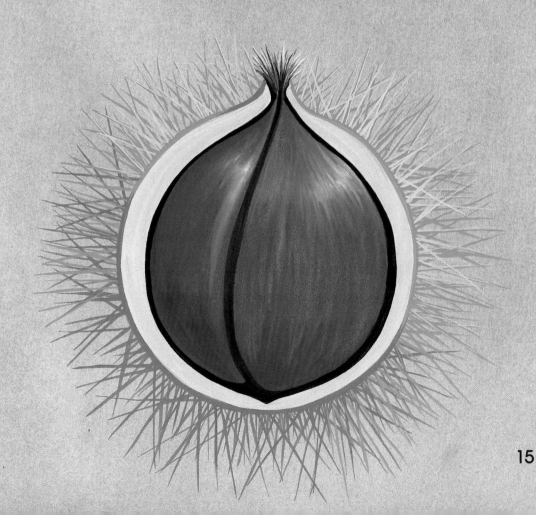

The chestnuts fall out of the bur.

In the autumn the burs drop to the ground. The case splits open and the brown, shiny chestnuts fall out. The leaves of the chestnut tree change color from deep green to yellow, orange and brown. They fall to the ground and protect the chestnuts.

Many chestnuts are eaten by animals.

Chestnuts are good to eat. People collect them to use in food or to roast and eat. Animals like to eat chestnuts, too. They may also store them to eat later. This means that many chestnut seeds will not grow into new trees.

Chestnuts under the ground in the winter.

Some of the chestnut seeds will grow into new trees. The chestnuts lie under the ground for at least one winter. They will not start to grow until the soil gets warmer.

21

Chestnuts in the spring.

In the spring a tiny **root** will begin to grow out of the chestnut. The root will grow down into the ground. It will hold the plant in the ground when it begins to grow. The root takes in water and food from the soil to help the chestnut grow.

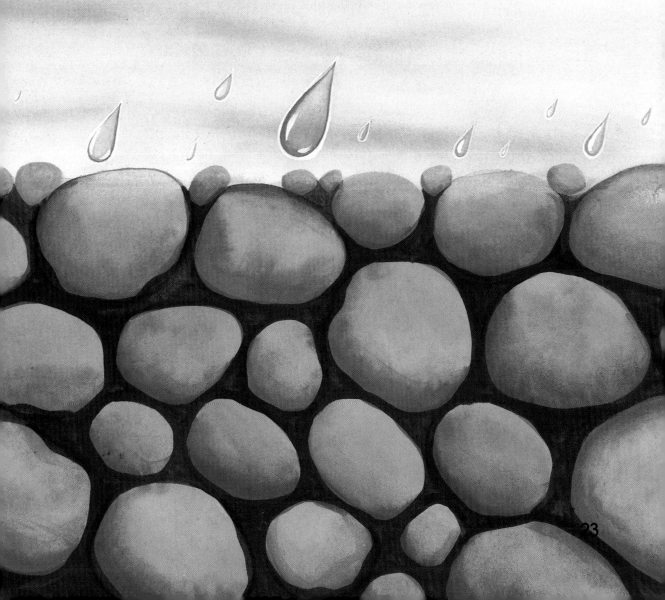

Chestnuts grow out of the ground.

After a few weeks a tiny **shoot** will appear above the ground. This shoot grows from the part of the root that is nearest the chestnut. One year later the shoot will have grown about six green leaves and will be fifteen centimeters (6 inches) high.

25

Full-grown chestnut trees.

It will be a very long time before a chestnut shoot becomes a full-grown tree. Every spring the chestnut tree will grow male and female catkin flowers. What do you think will happen then?

Chestnut and apple pudding.

You will need:
8 oz unsweetened chestnut purée
1/4 cup confectioners sugar
2/3 cup apple juice
2/3 cup whipped cream
2 egg whites
about 2 oz prepared meringues

Put the chestnut purée in a bowl with the sugar and stir with a wooden spoon until the mixture is smooth. Add the apple juice, a bit at a time, and beat this until it is all mixed in and looks smooth and soft. Cover the bowl with foil and put it in the freezer until the mixture has become stiff.

Take the bowl out of the freezer and **fold in** the whipped cream. Beat the egg whites until they are white and fluffy and fold them into the mixture. Lastly, break the meringues up with your fingers and fold them into the chestnut cream. Cover the bowl again and put it back into the freezer until it becomes firm. Now it is ready to eat.

The life cycle of a chestnut tree.

How many stages of the life cycle can you remember?

Glossary

Bark The outer covering of a tree.

Burs Burs hold the seeds while they are growing. They have thick, hard skins, which split open when the seeds are ready to come out.

Catkins The long, thin parts of a chestnut tree that grow male and female flowers.

Fertilization The moment when the pollen joins with parts of the female flower. Together they will make new seeds.

Fold in To mix in cream or another kind of food by carefully turning the mixture at the bottom of the bowl over the mixture at the top with a spoon. This slowly mixes in the cream without losing the thickness of the mixture.

Pollen A fine powder made by most flowers. Pollen is needed to make new seeds.

Pollination Taking the pollen from one flower to another to make a seed.

Root The part of a plant that grows down into the ground and takes in water and food to help it grow.

Shoot The shoot is the first part of a plant to grow out of the ground.

Finding out more

Here are some books to read to find out more about trees.

Biology: Plants, Animals and Ecology by
    Ifor Evans (Franklin Watts, 1984)
Trees by Carolyn Boulton (Franklin Watts,
    1984)
Trees by Martyn Hamer (Franklin Watts,
    1983)
Trees of the World by David Lambert
    (Bookwright Press, 1986)

Index